Muttertongue

what is a word in utter space

m.tut.ter.ongue

what is a word in utter space

Lillian Allen
Gary Barwin
Gregory Betts

Afterword by Kaie Kellough

EXILE editions

singular fiction, poetry, nonfiction, translation, drama, and graphic books

THE RATCATCHER POETRY SERIES: BOOK ONE

Library and Archives Canada Cataloguing in Publication

Title: Muttertongue : what is a word in utter space / Lillian Allen, Gary Barwin,
    Gregory Betts ; afterword by Kaie Kellough.
Names: Allen, Lillian, 1951- author | Barwin, Gary, author | Betts, Gregory,
    1975- author | Kellough, Kaie, 1975- writer of afterword
Description: Series statement: The ratcatcher poetry series ; book 1
Identifiers: Canadiana (print) 2024045894X | Canadiana (ebook) 20240458990 |
    ISBN 9781990773389 (softcover) | ISBN 9781990773396 (EPUB) |
    ISBN 9781990773402 (Kindle) | ISBN 9781990773419 (PDF)
Subjects: LCGFT: Spoken word poetry.
Classification: LCC PS8551.L5554 M88 2024 | DDC C811/.54 — dc23

Book designed by Michael Callaghan & Muttertongue Trio
Cover designed by Gary Barwin
Typeset in Bembo font at Moons of Jupiter Studios
Printed and Bound in Canada by Gauvin

Published by Exile Editions ~ www.ExileEditions.com
144483 Southgate Road 14, Holstein, Ontario, N0G 2A0

We gratefully acknowledge the Government of Canada and Ontario Creates
for their financial support toward our publishing activities.

We warmly thank Aetna Pest Control (Toronto) for their ongoing support.

Canadian sales representation: The Canadian Manda Group, 664 Annette Street,
Toronto ON M6S 2C8 www.mandagroup.com 416 516 0911

North American and international distribution, and U.S. sales:
Independent Publishers Group, 814 North Franklin Street,
Chicago IL 60610 www.ipgbook.com toll free: 1 800 888 4741

The layerings of sounds, languages, embodiment and reconfiguration of meaning, poetics, beingness is at the heart of an endless reshaping, refashioning of the world. This is what we have done, this is what we will always do. This remaking of what is essentially human is the vanguard of the cool. —TRACIE MORRIS, *Who Do With Words*

A MUTTER OF PROSE: TRIAL BY TRIALOGUE

Over the course of a year or two, and building from a decade and more of conversations, we three came together to explore the space between oral cultures, orality, language, dub, sound and semiotic-sonic play, working from a provocative premise that post-colonial and decolonizing forces in/against Canada are themselves a leading edge in avant-garde sonic literary expression and can be aligned with avant-garde experiments with language, coding and decoding, and pushing into new territories for poetic expression across cultures. We explored sound and sense and silence and nonsense on the stage, in the sound studio, and then down in the chambers of Orin Isaac's gorgeous recording sensorium. We set our thinking about language and its role in shaping who we are to music, thinking about how words help and hinder us as we struggle to become ourselves, how we end up muttering ourselves into being, uttering ourselves from mud, from mothers, from so many things only partially heard, partially mapped. We wondered about the silences. We captured our experimentation with the frame of an LP (from Siren Recordings) and then playfully wrestled text, images and evocations onto the pages for this book. There is nothing passive or limited about the page: we sought the leap, the siege, and the daring stage for a vibrant, visual interruption. Each letter is a scene. Each scene an act of utterance. We wanted to see the page come alive in all its rich, sonorous, exquisite mutterance.

Lillian: What are stored in sounds?

Most days I don't feel like talking. I'm really a mumbler. I delight myself with my own moans and groans and hummings daily. Enunciation might be habit but it's unnatural work for me, I practice. It's like I have to call upon certain cells in my body for a language presentation of syntax and affect in formal and semiformal contexts. I can feel the colonizing effect of language; the English language moving me away from embodiment. Hanging with my granddaughter when she was too young to speak, her sounds remind me that sounds exist outside of language; the languages we know. There is a mystery to sound. The gesture of breath into sound is primordial. Sound holds magic.

Who are we to ourselves before language?

"Come soon, mama soon come, soon come, mama come soon…" I was singing a lullaby spontaneously arising from my attempting to sway and comfort my granddaughter, in the Jamaican vernacular. Will this take root in her skin as cultural heritage? Where will this specific cultural ideophonic expression be stored? Will it be stored in her brains, her mind, her soul, her body?

Gary: So what are we doing in these recordings and in this book? These are jam sessions. Language jams. Loggish jams. Luggage jams. Our way of mediating our work, our way of finding our place in the language, in the world of language creation. How do we talk about what we talk about? What register to register what we register? But it is this coming together from different perspectives that makes collaboration so interesting for me, whether in a discussion such as this, in our printed poems, or in our recorded work.

In my case, over the last few years I have been exploring language and my cultural heritage, mostly through Hebrew/Yiddish letterforms and using Yiddish words. Other than a learned-early ability to say the "ch" gutteral sound in Channukah, I don't have any particular expertise with the sounds of my ancestors. I do shrug and gesticulate when I adopt a Yiddish-inflected register. So, you want I explain the metaphysical significance of the Hebrew alphabet? And, let me tell you, since I'm such a maven, how Yiddish is saturated in a particular world-view and historical experience. How I'm realizing that I feel it in my spine, this mamaloshen, this smotheredtongue that was the language of my grandparents, my father-in-law and his mother, and which I've heard since childhood as if listening from my bed to the adults' party.

Gregory: My parents spoke English comfortably, and their parents did as well. Going back one generation further, though, we have Gaelic in our roots from there – only two or three generations removed back to time immemorial. Some came from Scotland, viciously cleared from the Highlands in a manner somewhat analogous to what the Scottish, led by Macdonald, did to the Indigenous people once they arrived in Canada. The cycles of violence are plain and gross. Other sides of the family, going back a full two centuries now, came from Ireland, chased out of there in a similar manner. I guess as a result of that distance and that history, I have never felt any drive to re-engage with my linguistic heritage. And yet, when I was living in a Gaelic space – with my kids bringing home new Irish words everyday – the language (its rhythms, its cadence, its subtle dance) filled up my psychic environment. Dad, your srón is leaking. Please buille do shrón.

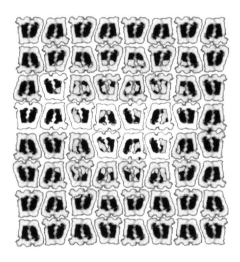

Gary: I experience Yiddish bodily, fully aware of the disembodied voices of my grandparents' families, silenced in the Shoah. And the letterforms take me back to my experience of the numinous perceptual asemia of the synagogue and Hebrew-school prayerbook, a world which could be written with such glyphs, such ancient orthographic navigations into an older world beyond the material. I sense I'm carrying these letters like alefbetic DNA beneath my skin, locating myself in the world through the seen lattice of these letters, even though I'm not able to speak or read the tongue they (m)utter.

Lillian: I often think about language as this inadequate thing that we use to both access and create communication and culture, as we try to counter this

very deep-seated human insecurity that no one truly knows and understands us. As if we even know ourselves! Is it the language we tell ourselves about ourselves? Is it how we try to make sense of experience? Or is it our experience that solidifies language? I'm riffing here because of course, we're trapped in the groove we call (Canadian) English expressed at a certain register. But really I'm personally bored with this very narrow mode of communication, I find it a bit claustrophobic! Not that I want to say "*uck it!" or anything like that. That's still English, except *uck it! is now a sprawling punctuation (mark) or invictive vocalizing an emotion. Where do we put some of that stuff that language just can't grasp? So, I'm also interested in how one makes oneself visible and present against Empire as Larissa Lai would describe it. As our poem asks "what is a word"?!!! I'm thinking of how we are all stuck in our own language, not just the words, though words are such suckers for their limitations, mere approximation and power to colonize with abstractions. Are we stuck in language, the language in our head? The common language of work, family and community? Academic language…? Like maybe… maybe like how we are stuck in our skin, and I mean this as a container/containment. bill bissett used to say, "don't mess with language, even if you're not saying anything, people get very very upset." Is language like a cult? A currency for white civility? Can language decolonize, allow us to step outside social history and the colonial gaze? Re-chart possible futures? Can it shift social relations?

Perhaps collaboration raises an intrinsic question that speaks to something larger, "is 'the other' knowable?" and then begs the follow-up question, "is that even a worthy pursuit?" The question that comes up for me is how little we know of the other. Is it possible to know more about the other through ...okay, let's make a list... together.... Dialogue? Collaboration? Literature? Music? Book learning? Intimacy? Repeated interactions? Play? Friendship? Struggling together? Allyship? Sharing power? Parsing privilege? Mmmm.....??? Is there a field beyond "otherness," perhaps a field of positionalities? Could creative collaboration contribute to this field? What is it that we are reaching for? Is it connection...? A personal ability to own space and time? Emergence, ritual, community, or is it transcendency that we seek?

Okay, back to sound and language; that vocalization of thoughts and emotion; "sound as sight, images as sound. Language is a skin the blanket we live in." Musicality, orality, vernacular riddims. As far as language goes, are we erasing something when we work with sounds or are we reinscribing possibilities? Or are we entering a new portal?

Question to you Greg. I noticed how active and vocal your kids are. We are all grown up and kinda sophisticated and have set our knowledge in theories about sound and literary sound poetics. Theories aside, I wonder if you can reflect on what your children are teaching you about voice and sound as a duo?

Gregory: If nothing else, my kids constantly remind me of our different positions in language. They are coming into it, surprised by it, and sometimes naturally suspicious of the tricks adults use with words – idioms, mannerisms, euphemisms, white lies. I may say something that seems clear enough to me, a phrase or idiom that I take for granted, but if my words don't perform in their headspace, they hear something else entirely. We are learning to talk to each other, across the slippage of language, where we all seem driven by a desire to make the words say different things to different ears. And they need the vitality of the world encoded in words – not just what it is, but how it came to be. Stories! Dynamic stories! What makes the dead things shine within the present. We look at what is in the world, ancient monuments, for instance, and think through them together, reaching toward a language that brings them to life. This old stone was *carved*. How could it have been carved before bronze? Who were the people? We can step back together and look at the thing without it pointing directly into their (or my) me me me me me, and branding the world as already made without them. That's a small example, but we really do make an effort to talk about what we are hearing in each other's words.

I guess, language for me is like a lightning spark between two electric bodies. (And not necessarily living bodies.) That blue bolt that passes between us. It connects us to each other, but it can hurt, too, can leave a scar, and it can just as easily signal distance and error as provide a bridge or succour to the other.

Gary: So Greg, in what place does language place you? What memories of mothertongue have made you, located you in your locutions? During your year in Ireland, did you hear the language in a new way, were you reminded  of Englishes, of the Eire of its ways, of its sounds and lilts, regions and divergences, of its portrayals and place?

Gregory: I thought I had no special connection to Ireland, except that I was there. I got lulled into a sense of luxury of familiarity (it is so gentle, easy, kind, welcoming, cool, green) and then BAM! Completely disorienting. When I speak to people there, I notice their rhythm is different, they turn a little closer when they speak, listen a little harder. They have more time for flushing out the language. Even the signs! Instead of our economical "No corkage," for instance, a restaurant near us had paid for a more mannered message: "You are quite welcome to bring your own bottle with your meal." They pay for each letter of that sign! And what they are paying for is a humanization of the person reading it, a gesture of recognition. Like a balm for the brute bolt of exchange.

My 5yo sang to herself in Irish. A dream in a foreign tongue.

These layers all overlap and intersect and make speaking really hard. What I do with my kids, as we work to be together with and without all that baggage, as we revel in learning the foibles of language, and ourselves in that house of language, is to declare spaces of play with words, of speaking sometimes only through error. Maybe it is pure babble, maybe it is silly phrases, most often it is badly misremembered song lyrics bastardized into comic absurdities. But we have a way, now, of signalling to each other that we want relief from the pressure cooker of words. We use unhinged words to giggle together and create sparks, sparkles of imagination. As bpNichol once said, this is "serious play." And this might be what happens when you read *Finnegans Wake* to your newborn, which is the great Irish riverrunning through it all.

Lillian: Signal, signifying, code switching. Searching for self in language, a secret passage, an adventure, not retreating but reaching. My mother's tongue is not her own. Her mother's tongue was not her own and neither was her mother's mother.

Gary: I'll mark a return of my own volleyition here, coz I've been thinking. I waxed Waynificiently about the near mystic magical and cultural properties of language above or before (depending on if you read pagespace as time or space and assuming directionality – i.e. we're *down* here now, *later* than before and I wrote this further down and later. Maybe this was the first thing on the page. Although the pages are only virtual images of pages on a computer screen. Reader, I'm not sure, as of yet, how you are reading this. And the conflagration of the world? How was it? Wished I could have been there instead of, y'know, here.) But anyway. We're talking here. We were.

I wanted to say that language isn't to be trusted. Or at least, don't trust its silvertongued inky-black duplicitous illusions to be more than the delightful play/ploy of signs and wonders. It's the braided rope that isn't there that yet gives us enough rope to hang ourselves on our hope of being able to pull ourselves up by our own bootstraps, to upbraid ourselves, to throw a line between ourselves and our minds, our minds and others. Our othertongue. It's quicksilver. Its slickquiver palaver wool-pullsover our I's often and supplants us with it and its rope-braids of smoke. Poof! And our essence wrestles with whatever it was before this magic hat trick.

But I've mostly been speaking about written language, about the author-graphic. Let's talk about anothertongue, an authortongue, the ontonguel-ogical reality of speech. Maybe it's more epistonguemological. Sometimes it feels like we speak a parallel world into existence or see the world through what we say, what we can say, what is said, including tripping on the tonguet-ricksters our language creates.

What do you think, Lillian & Greg? What is, for you, the difference between the written and the spoken, the oral and the scribal, and, while we're at it, between the linguistic and the paralinguistic – the otheredtongue?

Lillian: Oh the spoken, the glorious spoken. The first and the last. Not the broken or the token. I would say the spoken offers an embodied form of direct interactive communication that includes "extralingustic" features and can be played extemporaneously like music storing things we can never lose if our computer dies. It calls for presence and reminds us that we live in a relational world, in the now. It can create ritual and community. I like how sounds connects us beyond words and disrupts our sense of meaning and presuppositions. Everything in this world lies on a spectrum within a circle, interconnected; from before the silence, to the silence and right through to the din and beyond.

To your other point Gary, do we speak a parallel world into existence or are we existing in different worlds and speak it? Is the tongue our measure of reality? The tonguetricksters???

Poof! Houdini, Caliban, Solomon, Trickster, Miss Lou, Anancy. Magicmagu-politico. Grim Reaper.

In the US leaders are prone to characterizing elections as a battle for the soul of America. Where is this battle fought? Is language the battle-ground?

"Facku tum tum tum Facku tum tum tum…" to quote Gary.

Gregory: What about the play between sound poetry and dub poetry? Are these different worlds, battlegrounds, or is the avant-garde a space of meeting?

Lillian: When we talk about the avant-garde, generally writers of colour are excluded, not mentioned in so-called CanLit. We don't generally acknowledge that there are manifestations of different poetics across different cultural spaces. The British/Euro-imperial hierarchy is in full regalia and this we have to change.

My favourite sound poem is by Bob Marley, his scream that starts "Crazy Baldhead,": "oAoA oAo AoAoA!" (can't write this one down, the emotional intensity is off the charts). Every element of his song is contained in that sound. In fact, his entire anti-imperialism, anti-oppression, and calling for truth and justice is embedded in that one sound! It is a sonic eruption against oppression and imperialist forces. Another poem I admire for its performative sound expression is "Chuckie Prophesy" by Canadian Dub poet Clifton Joseph. The poem's persona, Chuckie, is an ordinary young black man in the throes of discovering that chasing the elusive and expensive American dream is becoming his nightmare, and so he is a grassroots insurrectionary in the making. The poem starts with "shum ma de ma nede dela naddy na dow." In the same way that Dub Poetry is rooted in meaning, in transforming language and registers of language as a decolonizing practice, the poem works with sound elements and its powerful emotive quality in performance/vocalization to signify and underscore resistance. Two other poems of Clifton Joseph's are off the charts for me as literary sonic enterprises. His poem for Coltrane is a highly crafted drawl meandering wordless bawling through sounds that would clear a funeral parlour. His poem for Monk combines stylized vocal soundings of Monk's tinkling notes, treating them like phonemes, delighting and surprising us. My poem, "Rub a Dub Style inna Regent Park," begins with an emergency; no words, just an elongated sound!

Dub poetics are attuned to the rhythmic life of the word. You break language and words into the possible rhythmic elements and utilize voice and vocalization to stylize and create an aesthetic. This allows for an audial recoding, for formation of new auditory cultural codes and an aesthetic that is also culturally aligned mixing and combining different cultural modes. There is a reach for a register that will unify and create new sites of cultural connectivity. When I return to Jamaica, my use of language and vernacular are not registered as Jamaican because they hear the foreign (the Canadian, so to speak) in me, but my work (especially in the early days) isn't registered in Canada as Canadian because they hear the Jamaican in me and also hear me as foreign.

The avant-garde has given me another container to look to and draw from. In the contemporary Canadian context, mixing and meshing, giving and taking and forging new alliances. My "Birth Poem," for example, is both contemporary and primordial and is about a universal experience that is just not languageable. You have to go right back to pre-language to even begin to enter that experience. It has to be language that you are swimming in to shape an expression that could evoke and bring people back to their own primal encounter with birth. A poem like this ends up being in the same place as the avant-garde. Dub sees itself as avant-garde, rushing the gates, trampling walls, calling for voice and a unity against oppression. An empowering repositioning of the term. A call for revolution. Frankly, in today's world, in contemporary society, we BIPOC folks don't ascribe too much political intention to the literary avant-garde of today. We don't believe in just imagining imaginings and play on the page. Instead, we want bodies on the line standing against injustice, with us. And standing up for values of equality in your own spheres, especially when we are not looking! We want to see some divestment of some of that white privilege too.

Yes, I understand the historical literary impulse, and of course, the dastardly oppressive military realities from which the term "avant-garde" originated. But what we (in my cultural milieu) love about the literary avant-garde is what we see as a kind of "brattishness" that comes with privilege. I had a similar feeling when I first saw the Clichettes, the all-woman feminist performing arts group in the late '70s in Toronto. I figured oh sattamassagana! Somebody is burning Daddy's house down! So with the literary avant-garde, it wasn't necessarily politics but instead we saw these white guys affronting white middle-class civility and decorum in literature, ignoring sacred rules (ask an immigrant) and mocking formalities. How uncouth! But how joyful! And as these writers loosen their straitjackets and bust up neatly tied-up boundaries and jump across creative forms, that is where we meet. Regarding collaborations, the Métis artist David Renault told me that the system from which each is operating must be disturbed possibly even creating ruptures to be able to formulate something that belongs not to one but to all of us. But still the hierarchy of what is seen and respected as important work in our literary and artistic culture must be confronted.

Gregory: Our work is grounded in each of our languages, other languages, our language, in different ways. Our practice and interest overlap, complement and also depart from each other in different ways. We discovered much commonality (and laughter) in the ways of the testing and pushing language space.

Gary: Here's sumthin to summon, summa, summerize and light it up:

> *Celan told himself, in German:*
> *"this word is your mother's ward*
> *your mother's ward stoops for the crumb of light."*
> —ILYA KAMINSKY

...

MUTTER APPROACHES THE SPEED OF LIGHT

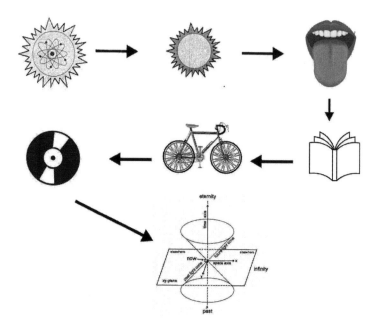

I'm taking a breath here

                  hence the blank page

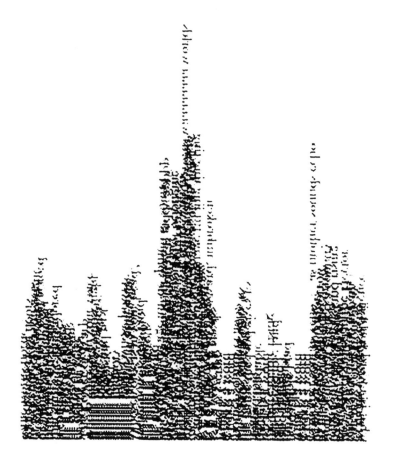

14

What is a Word You Use

what is a word you use
to speak through old silence
as mother sounds echo

you may come from away
but of your folding in pain
what is a word you use

they sailed stuffed in the Hector
cleared o' Lochbroom
as mother sounds echo
from fo'c'sle to boom
before an unreadable land rising
what is a word you use

such Scots that birthed a country
in the image of Gaelic sorrow
as mother sounds echo
in the lash of Old Tomorrow
peace, order, old horrors
what is a word you use
as mother sounds echo

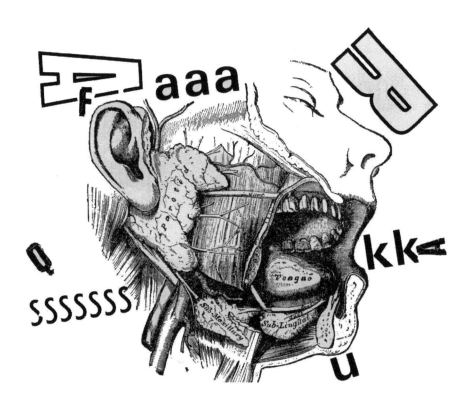

The Tongue is Not in Exile

It is the voice you use
It is the voice you use

Before a violet world
It is the voice you use

Before fire
It is the voice you use

Before red morning
Before blue night

It is the voice you use
It is the voice you use

Before mouth, before struggle
Before before

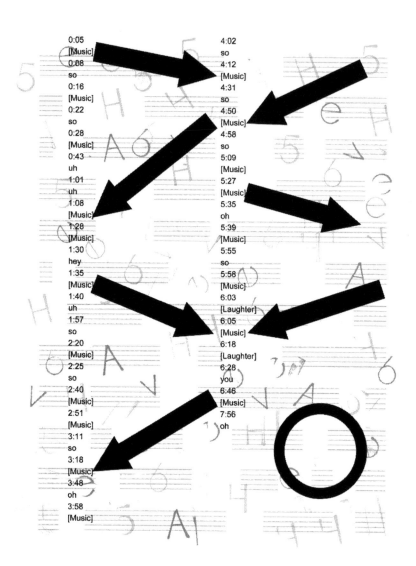

as mother sounds echo

                    what is a word
                         a word
                  what is a word
                  word
                  what is a word

                  readable
              unreadable
          the reading land
              the unreadable
                      land rising
                           the readable
                  land rising
              the unreadable land
                  rising
          the unreadable rising

              what is a word
                      the land
                           rising
                                    what is readable
                                    unreadable
                                              rising

                           the name the land gives us
                           the names we carry
                           the words which carry us
                           the names which carry us
                           as mother sounds echo
                           mother sounds echo

          what is a word
                  a word
                      what is a word
                      word
              what is

Lullababy / Lallubaby

Woken & Unbroken

Woken & Unbroken

Is it a voice if it speaks
    Is it a voice if it creaks
        Is it a voice if it lays wayward, unbroken
        Is it an immigrant thang
        Is it a land yearning
    Is it blood in the land soaking

Woken & Unbroken

Is it a restorative thing
    Is it a justice riddim
            In lands of broken and the stolen
            Is it a voice if it's AI
    Whose God give it a voice
And must it always speak white
                            Speak white
                                Speak white
What of the token word
        What of the broken word
            What of the broken word
                What of the token word

Woken & Unbroken

                    Yes, it's a voice if it squeaks
            Resistance its speaks
        Revolution it teach   te ee ch es

Woken & Unbroken
        Woken & Unbroken

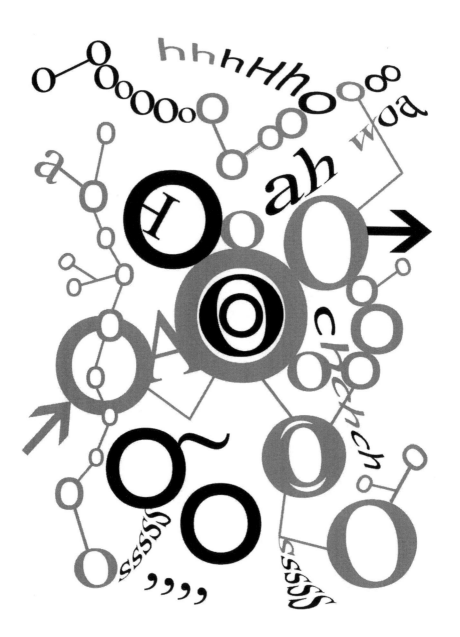

Voices in the Land

This land
on which we stance
Is generous
This land in us, genius
This land Indigenous
restores us

Violence hidden in colonial tongues
troll human rights
In whose voice must we fight
On the road to decolonize

this deep underground
Language & Land, alight,

erasure de sound
Erasure de voice
de sound in the body

an' de spirit in the land
an' de sound in ideas
and sound of lie
de token word
de broken word

dis land dis land dis landing
dis land in us   is us
dis land is generous
   dis land indigenous
restores us
Indigenous is this Land

Indigenous this Land

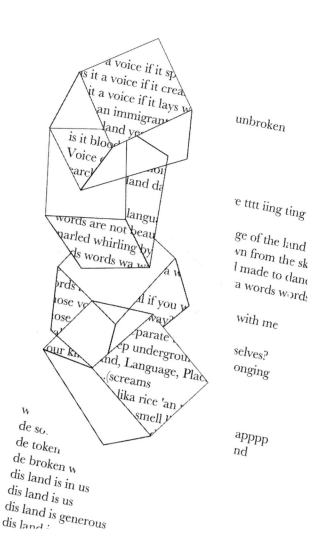

it a voice it 1
, it a voice if i
s it an immigi
s it a land yea
s it blood in t
Voice echos,
searching a la

the land of a
words are n
snarled whi
words word
worlds
words are
whose voi
whose voi
breaking
in our kii
Speak w
Mi say n
like whe
when y
de sour
de toke
de bro
dis lar
dis lai
dis la
dis la
dis la

a voice if it sp
s it a voice if it crea
it a voice if it lays w
an immigran
and ye
is it blood
Voice
arc
land da

unbroken

langu
words are not beau
narled whirling by
ds words wa w

e tttt iing ting

ge of the land
vn from the sk
l made to danc
a words words

rds
ose v
ose
a v
l if you
vay?
parate
p undergrou
nd, Language, Plac
(screams
lika rice 'an
smell

with me

selves?
onging

w
de so.
de token
de broken w
dis land is in us
dis land is us
dis land is generous
dis land

apppp
nd

The map   your tongue

          marked   by diagrams

constellations   (r)   evolving

breath making sounds;

             probes into muther space

                              an eclipse that breaks orbit

against empire

     (re) inscribing a possibility for a new order

sub verbal   hyper vocal

                    new alphabet throated   emotive registers
language sounds

rotated

             spectral observatory

utterances

     galaxies   from the mouth

fact factual   fractal fractured   filament of firmament   word clatter

splatter dark   matter   celestial language chatter

                                        pitched peaks where rivers of
belonging once flower

Dem use to sew, he sey, she sey, we sey

Would you please split that atom

Down to its last syllable   ssss lllll la bb bl e

then splice   remix   spice

                            flow songic to poetry

phonemes alive poetics to sounds, like de sap inside a tree trickkle

riddim life

styling

mimic the invisible

                                breath to gesture

Once silent invisible jester   in body and space

                             & now poetic probes into utter space

    poetic probes inna utter space

Whose voice is in your head?

whose head is in your voice
　　whose land is in your voice
　　　　whose body is in your voice
　　　　　　whose words whose power
　　　　　　whose song
　　　　　　　　whose money
　　　　　　　　　　whose memory
　　　　　　　　　　　　whose hope
　　　　　　　　　　　　　　whose anger
　　　　　　　　　　　　　　　　whose love
　　　　　　　　　　　　　　　　　　whose confusion
　　　　　　　　　　　　　　　　　　　　whose
　　　　　　　　　　　　　　　　future and past
　　　　　　　　　　　　　　whose dance
　　　　　　　　　　　　　whose brother & sister
　　　　　　　　　　　whose father & mother
　　　　　　　　　whose darkness whose light
　　　　　　　whose alphabet
　　　　　whose voice is in your voice

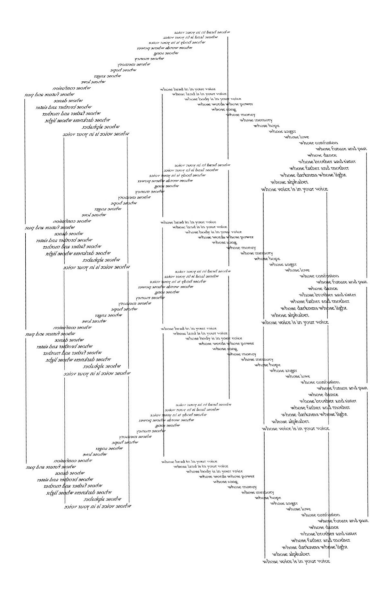

whose head
is in your
voice whose
land is in
your voice
whose body
is in your
voice whose
words
whose
power
whose song
whose
money
whose
memory
whose hope
whose
anger
whose love
whose
confusion
whose
future and
past whose
dance
whose
brother &
sister whose
father &
mother
whose dark-
ness whose
light whose
life, death,
alphabet
whose voice
is in your
voice

whose headwhose headwhose head
is in youris in youris in your
voice whosevoice whosevoice whose
land is inland is inland is in
your voiceyour voiceyour voice
whose bodywhose bodywhose body
is in youris in youris in your
voice whosevoice whosevoice whose
wordswordswords
whosewhosewhose
powerpowerpower
whose songwhose songwhose song
whosewhosewhose
moneymoneymoney
whosewhosewhose
memorymemorymemory
whose hopewhose hopewhose hope
whosewhosewhose
angerangeranger
whose lovewhose lovewhose love
whosewhosewhose
confusionconfusionconfusion
whosewhosewhose
future andfuture andfuture and
past whosepast whosepast whose
dancedancedance
whosewhosewhose
brother &brother &brother &
sister whosesister whosesister whose
father &father &father &
mothermothermother
whose dark-whose dark-whose dark-
ness whoseness whoseness whose
light whoselight whoselight whose
life, death,life, death,life, death,
alphabetalphabetalphabet
whose voicewhose voicewhose voice
is in youris in youris in your
voicevoicevoice

The Power of Warp

words or swords or warps or worse   or draws or verse   or wards or war   or dreams or seams
or a mess of sores or a dress of chords or a step of doors or a press of chores a confession's scores
this far flung shore that ship's've long adored   punctuate misreading   punctuation bleeding
like funiculì or funiculà or funicular words rise of their own accord   a cable for your thoughts
or what isn't already bought in fact contact was an act we parenthesized some words close doors

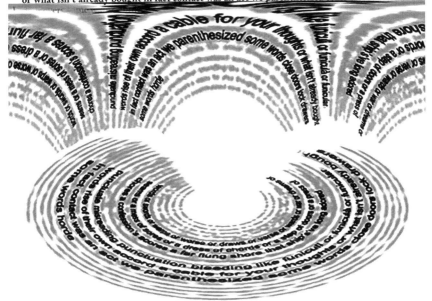

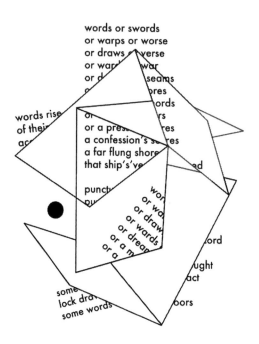

words or swords
or warps or worse
or draws or verse
or war wor
or d seams
res
ords
words rise rs
of thei res
a or a pre res
a confession's s res
a far flung shore
that ship's've ad

punct
 wor
or wo
or draw
or wards
or drea
or a m
or a

ord

ught
act
some
lock dra
some words ors

Throwt Ice

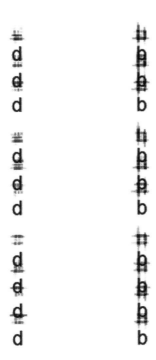

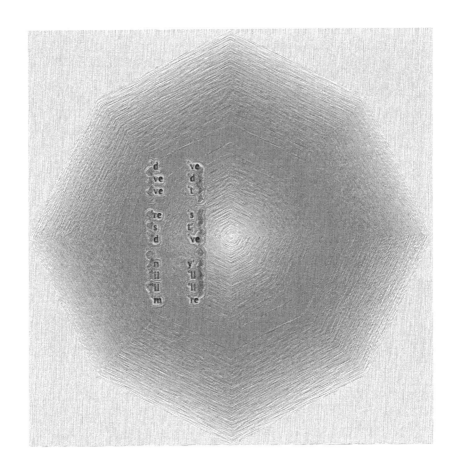

Accent without Leave

what is a voice a what is a voice a what is a voice a

voice what is a voice what is a voice what is a

voice voice what is voice voice what is voice voice what is

a voice spoken un- a voice spoken un- a voice spoken un-

spoken the spoken spoken the spoken spoken the spoken

land the unspoken- land the unspoken- land the unspoken-

land rising the land rising the land rising the

spoken land rising spoken land rising spoken land rising

the unspoken land the unspoken land the unspoken land

rising the unspoken rising the unspoken rising the unspoken

rising what is a rising what is a rising what is a

voice the land voice the land rising voice the land

what is spo- what is spoken un- what is spo-

spoken risi- spoken rising the spoken ris-

name the land giv- name the land gives name the land gives

us the names we us the names we us the names we

carry the voices carry the voices carry the voices

which carry us the which carry us the which carry us the

names which carry names which carry names which carry

us as mother us as mother us as mother

sounds echo sounds echo sounds echo

mother sounds mother sounds mother sounds

echo what is a voice echo what is a voice echo what is a voice

a voice what is a a voice what is a a voice what is a

voice voice what is voice voice what is voice voice what is

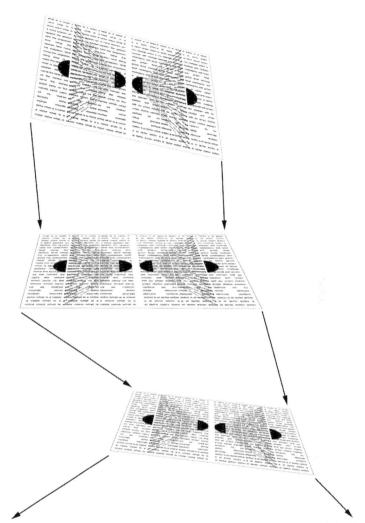

Soon Flower

                                        a pale hashtag
                                    shrouded in snow
                                blackbirds rising
            in graves' flight

        take this broken laugh and learn flight

        all these white-legged sunflowers
rioting against time

            you were waiting
                to give life but you must make life
            upon the billion-blooded sea
                    sparrow what did you do to me

        I was a blackbird with sunflower wings
                    it sat beside me, unholy thing

                            I   travelled to where speaking   shrouds
                    I parked my   car and looked at stars

            I did not   move
    I flew   through time

                            my blood was voice
                            and I remained
                            silent

                                singing, like that

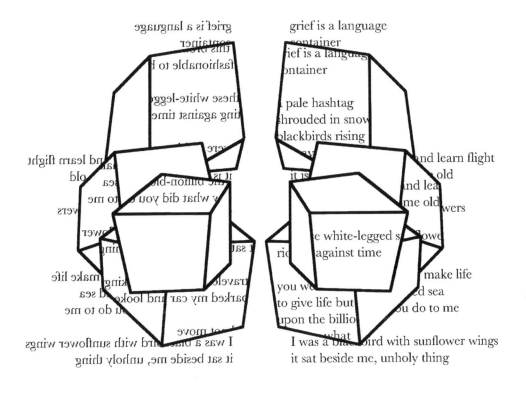

grief is a language
container
ief is a languag
ontainer

a pale hashtag
shrouded in snow
blackbirds rising

nd learn flight
old
nd lea
me old wers

e white-legged s owe
ri against time

make life
you w d sea
to give life but u do to me
upon the billio
what
I was a black bird with sunflower wings
it sat beside me, unholy thing

Bird

it
lurk
or cast
dark
it cauldron
morning

it glitter seas
hook or
dark heart

it arrow
or speak hard
it brindled wing

or blackbird sweet
it mutter
blood
it mouthfuls

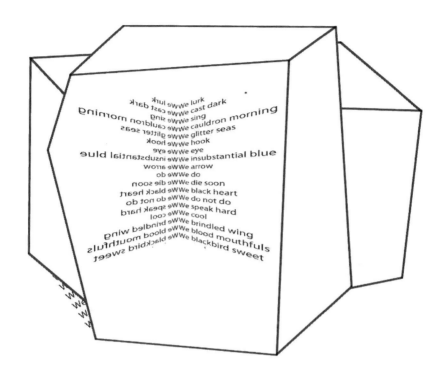

enJambling

Jambalaya

is what you feel

Jambaaling

Bee/\bop

paella

reggae/\rize

to tune

telephones

on the moon

on crust of de moon

hello hello halloa

can u hear mama moa

tuning

cacophonies into symphonies

from black holes to da blues

Ooh ooh ma chile

locating

What might this be

it
what is it
it is all
it is everything
it is
it is what you feel
it is the start of all things
it is the eye on the start
the turn back and the reflection that once
it wasn't

                              what was that like
                    just the question
what

then
suddenly
it

and from it all
it was, henceforward   what
it is

                         Woken &   you feel
                    after every
                         Unbroken
what

you feel the earth   Is it a voice if it speaks
is a what   Is it a voice if it creaks
you feel   ken   Is it a voice if it lays wayward, unbro-
each grain of sand   Is it an immigrant thang
is it   Is it a land yearning
                                Is it blood in the land soaking
other humans
is a what   ken & Unbroken
you feel storative thing
Is it
          Is it a justice riddim
              In lands of
broken and th

the stolen

Is it a voice if it's AI

Whose God give it a voice

And must it always speak white

Speak white   what happened to l

the body Speak white

is a what you feel

of the token word   it is how we deal with what

What of the broken word   the absence of we

broken word   What of the

token word   What of the

Woken & Unbroken

Yes, it's

a voice if it squeaks

speaks   Resistance its

Revolution it teach   te ee ch es

Woken & Unbroken

Woken & Unbro-

ken

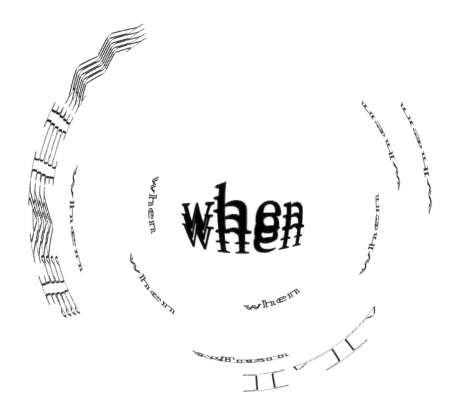

when
      when what became it
      when surrounded it
      wrench whence
      when what it once was
and what it might once be

      when never

Where

Where
    it was   my eye

that is
when   was and his or hers or theirs

who is also short
    for hope, the body of it
                who is always against here
    like when
    it is only
when it is not
        here

        like a body gone
        is suddenly who
why isn't it

why always when
why is never
        here
never here

never is what
    will hold a voice in place

for what you can't heal
        why was never at
why we couldn't find it
        why was never at the beach
even when once
        why was why we couldn't stop
it was here
        Looking

looking
looking
looking
looking
looking
looking
looking
looking
looking
looking

Still What

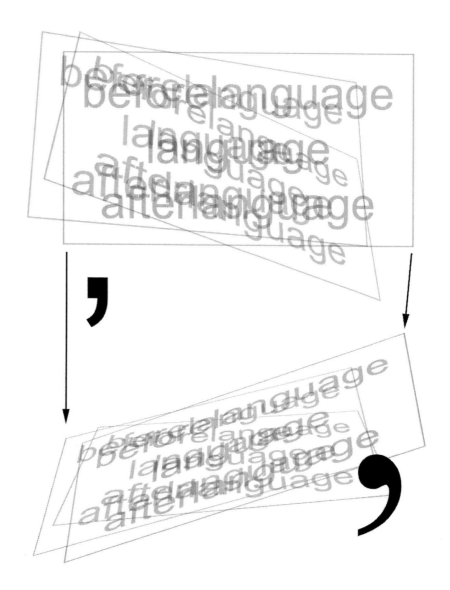

LissenIn

On Listening to Muttertongue

In this afterword, Kaie Kellough listens to the recording of Muttertongue. *This experience guides a consideration of the voices and sounds in this book. What are its rhythms and melodies? What are its voices and how do the voices interact? How does the page sound? The language(s)? How can we read with our ears, hear with our eyes?*

Silence in the headphones. In the muffled darkness of L and R, we hear a faint breath. That initial breath calls us to attention. It draws us outside the realm of words and into that of sounds, and yet it suggests speech, because breath is the material of voice. That breath fades up, until we hear one voice talking. That single voice, distinct, articulates a stream of words, smatterings of voice and other mouth-noise, dividing the silence with its sound.

A second voice starts talking. It talks over the first, now it drops to a whisper, and now it launches words and fragments of words at the same volume as the first. We can still distinguish one voice from the other, even though they overlap. In their overlap, words elongate and bend. Sometimes the words lose their shape altogether, and in the breath-borne elasticity of their vowels, they stretch into groans. Phonemes and morphemes are reshaped, then scattered. They rush and collide. No intentional meaning emerges from the collision. We imagine the voices magnetic, attracting and repelling one another. Now they yearn and reach out, they tangle, they push apart. We hear the space between them, and that space is quickly charged as a shout abrades a fricative.

A third voice announces itself, multiplying noise. The banter expands, while the encapsulating silence diminishes, but is re-established in moments – an accidental pause – and then overcome. The headphones are full, and the voices seem to tumble out of them and whirl around our heads. Even if each voice occupies a slightly different register than the others, the voices are no longer distinct. They momentarily blur. They become one another. It is difficult to tell how many people are talking. The syllables break and multiply, as do the subtle mouth sounds, the suck and whistle, the gnash and clack.

Sound poetry can expose the raw material of language. It can confirm that language is raw material. The poets on this record, Lillian Allen, Gary

Barwin, and Gregory Betts, improvise on breath and vocal sound, and create coherence using pauses, crescendos, alternations, and other techniques. We recognize words when no words are spoken. We hear the contours' familiar expressions. Their voices tug against language. They remind us that the sounds that have meaning for us are related to other sounds that don't. But then don't all sounds have meaning? Can't all vocal sounds potentially find a place in some language? One of the meanings may well be humour, and another may be exuberance. Even if the three poets are breathing and muttering, we sense joy mingling with effort. We hear the physicality of vocalization. We hear the body. We hear the body translated as sound. We hear echoes of land. We hear poetic instinct and poetic knowledge active in the body. We hear the strain and the immensity of utterance.

Within that immensity, the poets shape a space for improvisation. Spontaneous, they stretch utterances from breath to the recitation of words. Sometimes they fixate on a particular family of sounds, like those made when laughing or clearing the throat, but their improvisation never allows itself to settle, for too long, into an easy conversation.

A curious thing happens when three voices come together at once. Each one intervenes into the others, and the result is a splitting of voice into sounds and a remixing of those sounds into din. In a crowded room, or on a bus heading uptown we expect this, we even hear this as pleasant noise when it isn't too disruptive, because it gives a feeling of ambient babble, energy, it reassures.

Listening to a sound recording, our expectations shift. We often listen in a more purposeful way, we listen for something specific, a melody, a rhythmic pattern, a hook. We expect each vocal part to be distinct. When they overlap, not in harmony, not in rhythmic unison, but in the onrush of speech and speech-like utterance, the listener finds themselves inside that rush and wonders how to listen to it, what to listen for? Do we listen for words, or for how the shape of words easily shifts into a groan, or a sequence of loose vowels, or a rising, raucous shout? Do we listen to understand how close speech comes to complete incoherence? Can we calculate that distance? Do we listen for meaning? A narrative emotional subtext? A primal connectivity? How? No exclusive narrative emerges except that of overlap, interference. Nothing is linear or coherent. Word-fragments may be audible, stylized, but what do they add up to beyond exactly what they are: raw utterance? Or do we listen to the silence from which these sounds emerge?

In that interplay of sequencing and styling, interference, and overlap, we strive to hear the individual voice distinguish itself from the din, but instead one voice slides into another, identifies as the other. The I is elided, and in that moment we understand language not as eloquence, not as a performance of individual excellence, but as meshing and mingling, an experiment, a noisome articulation of collective striving. And then – just as we begin the hear the group dynamic, and we wonder if what we hear is cooperation or strife, suddenly one voice emerges: polished, identifiable, speaking, and we are reassured – before it too is swallowed by the babble.

—KAIE KELLOUGH, Montreal 2019/Sudbury 2024

THIS PROJECT IS BROUGHT TO YOU BY MUTTERTONGUE TRIO
ALLEN • BARWIN • BETTS

Lillian Allen

Gary Barwin

Gregory Betts

Lillian Allen is the City of Toronto's seventh Poet Laureate, and a longtime Creative Writing Professor at OCAD University, Toronto, where she founded a cross- and multi-disciplinary BFA creative writing program. She lectures and performs internationally, and publishes widely in print and in audio. She's a two-time Juno awards winner for her Dub Poetry with reggae music. In 2024, the Ontario Arts Council and The League of Canadian Poets established two Spoken Word awards named in her honour. Ms. Allen also received an honorary doctorate from Wilfrid Laurier University for her impact on Canadian Letters. Her current poetic practice pushes language to explore pre-language and post-language utterances, sound, and sonics in the formation and invention of new poetries. Her most recent written collection of poetry, *Make the World New* (Selected by Ronald Cummings), was published in 2021. www.LillianAllen.ca

Gary Barwin is a writer, multimedia artist, performer and musician, and the author of 32 books including *Scandal at the Alphorn Factory: New and Selected Short Fiction 2024-1984,* and the national bestselling novel *Yiddish for Pirates,* which won the Leacock Medal and the Canadian Jewish Literary Award, was a finalist for the Governor General's Award and the Giller Prize, and was long listed for Canada Reads. He was also shortlisted for the League of Canadian Poets' Spoken Word Award. His last novel, *Nothing the Same, Everything Haunted* was chosen as Hamilton Reads 2023. A PhD in music composition, his music, art, and writing have been performed, exhibited, published, and broadcast internationally. He lives in Hamilton, Ontario, Canada, and at Garybarwin.com. abcdefy.

Gregory Betts is a poet and professor at Brock University in St. Catharines, Ontario, Canada. His work consistently explores concrete, constrained, or collaborative poetics. He is the author of 11 books of poetry, including *BardCode* (2024), a visual rendering of the sound patterns in Shakespeare's sonnets. His poems have been stenciled into the sidewalks of St. Catharines, and selected by the SETI Institute to be implanted into the surface of the moon. He performed at the Vancouver 2010 Olympics, as part of the Cultural Olympiad, and has travelled and performed extensively across Canada, the U.S., and Europe. He is the curator of the bpNichol.ca Digital Archive, and author of the award-winning scholarly monographs *Finding Nothing: the VanGardes 1959-1975 and Avant-Garde Canadian Literature.*

Supporting cast

Kaie Kellough is a novelist, poet, and general word sound systemizer. He loves the anonymity of print and the dynamic physicality of sound. His electronic narratives unspool like a ribbon of magnetic tape.

Information on the Muttertongue recording

To experience the full sonic project, check out the recording *Muttertongue*, produced by Orin Isaacs – a genius producer and bass player extraordinaire. He is a composer of music for hit TV shows, a producer of Gold and Platinum selling records, and has musically directed some of the world's biggest artists. Nationally unknown as a trio, the Muttertongue posse is trying to slip unnoticed into those two last categories.

ACKNOWLEDGEMENTS

Left to Right: Orin Isaacs, Lillian Allen, Gary Barwin, Gregory Betts

The Niagara Artist Centre who hosted multiple performances, University College Dublin where we sang and muttered with full, open throats, OCAD University who support and host and let us launch into utter space, Kwong Chow where we jammed with TZT, Brock University, Orin Isaacs' Swing Low Studio (swinglow.ca), Ryan Barwin's Hazy Grove Studios, Sam Gottlieb, Tracie Morris, Siren Recordings, Deanna Radford, and a special shout out to Beatriz Hausner, Michael Callaghan and Gabriela Campos, and Barry Callaghan.

Photographs courtesy of: Sam Gottlieb (BHB) pages 1 and 57; Adam Dickinson page 8; Gregory Betts pages 4 and 6.